God's Decrees, Spoken By Me, I Receive!

Thank you Lord, for the increase!

LADY MARY HATTER

© Copyright 2018, Lady Mary Hatter

All Rights Reserved.

In accordance with the U.S. Copyright Act of 1976, the scanning, uploading, and electronic sharing of any part of this book without the permission of the publisher constitute unlawful privacy and theft of the author's intellectual property. If you would like to use material from the book (other than for preview purposes), prior written permission must be obtained by contacting the publisher at the address below. Thank you for your support of the author's rights.

ISBN: 978-1-948638-76-0

Dedication & Acknowledgement

To my husband, Pastor A.D. Hatter, Two children, Tangeneva, and Tristian. My granddaughter, Maranda, my grandson Josiah, both from my daughter Tangeneva. I love you all dearly.

I dedicate this book to all those who are reading and don't understand right now, this book is dedicated to you also. To all who read, I speak blessings to you indeed. My prayer is that you receive. This is my seed. I sow, so you will grow, and go, and that people will know. Continued blessings to the kingdom, and souls being saved. Blessings, blessings, and blessings always!

Introduction

I'm Excited, and Amazed, at the Awesomeness of God, once again, He allows us to win. He's given me another book to help us in receiving all His promises that's already been given us by grace through faith. This book came about when I decide to speak out my mouth what God had put on my mind and in my heart. My desire was to have the finer things in life as well as living for Him. I wanted to be blessed in my marriage, ministry, and money. I wanted my husband and I, our children, our family, and people of God to see and receive what God has promised. I asked God to allow me to be an example in the earth that He uses for the whole world to see, and they can say look what He's done, its marvelous in our sights. In other words, God show off in me!

THIS CAME ABOUT FROM THE LORD, AND IT IS MARVELOUS *and* WONDERFUL IN OUR EYES'?

MARK 12:11 AMP

The layout of this book came from listening to Apostle Leroy Thompson teaching on July 30, 2017. I thank God for His Apostle He's given to us. I gladly follow his instructions. I heard God say this is how you will present this book to help the body of Christ live in His ways for their lives. He said follow the instructions of the prophet. This is the scripture he took me to.

> I will raise up a prophet from among their countrymen like you, and I will put My words in his mouth, and he shall speak to them all that I command him.
>
> **DEUTERONOMY 18:18 AMP**

After He showed me this scripture He had me read from verse fifteen through twenty-two of this Chapter.

> The LORD your God will raise up for you a prophet like me [Moses] from among you, from your countrymen (brothers, brethren). You shall listen to him. This is according to all that you asked of the LORD your God at Horeb (Mount Sinai) on the day of the assembly, saying, 'Let me not hear the voice of the LORD my God again, nor see this great fire anymore, so that I will not die.' The LORD said to me, 'They have spoken well. ~'I will raise up a prophet from among their countrymen like you, and I will put My words in his mouth, and he shall speak

to them all that I command him. ~'It shall come about that whoever will not listen to My words which he shall speak in My name, I Myself will require it of him [and there will be consequences]. ~'But the prophet who presumes to speak a word in My name which I have not commanded him to speak, or which he speaks in the name of other gods—that prophet shall die.' If you say in your heart, 'How will we know and recognize the word which the LORD has not spoken?' When a prophet speaks in the name of the LORD and the thing does not happen or come true, that is the thing which the LORD has not spoken. The prophet has spoken it presumptuously; you shall not be afraid of him.

DEUTERONOMY 18:15-22 AMP

You will notice the Decrees are set up in a particular order, and you will have help in decreeing everything to you. **Again, God said, "this book will help The Body of Christ live in His ways for their lives."** Sometimes I like to use words easy to explain, and understand, by using the same letter words, acronyms, and initials.

Here are a couple of examples of how the Decrees are set up:

1) **Saved/Delivered and living in,**

2) **Sanctification/Divine** which is, oneness with God, choosing to move out of self, and into the one and

only solvent Saviour and Lord of our lives. You will not possess any of these decrees you speak except you give your life totally to Him and receive. Never forget to say thank you after each decree. Repent of your sins now, and ask God to come into your heart and save you. Confess this scripture out loud, and make Him proud. Receive your salvation and thank Him for it. I praise God for you now!

> Because if you acknowledge and confess with your mouth that Jesus is Lord [recognizing His power, authority, and majesty as God], and believe in your heart that God raised Him from the dead, you will be saved. For with the heart a person believes [in Christ as Savior] resulting in his justification [that is, being made righteous—being freed of the guilt of sin and made acceptable to God]; and with the mouth he acknowledges and confesses [his faith openly], resulting in and confirming [his] salvation. For the Scripture says, "WHOEVER BELIEVES IN H IM [whoever adheres to, trusts in, and relies on Him] WILL NOT BE DISAPPOINTED [in his expectations]." For there is no distinction between Jew and Gentile; for the same Lord is Lord over all [of us], and [He is] abounding in riches (blessings) for all who call on Him [in faith and prayer]. For " WHOEVER CALLS

ON THE NAME OF THE LORD [in prayer] WILL BE SAVED.

ROMANS 10:9-13 AMP

We must follow the BIBLE. Which is,

Believers

Instructions

Being

Led

Everyday.

We must keep all negativity and naysayers out of our way. When I learned about decrees I didn't want to keep them to myself. I wanted you to receive help. I invite you to be filled with Holy Spirit with the evidence of speaking in tongues. Now that you are saved, ask God to fill you with the overflow of His Spirit now, just like this scripture says. Make sure you say to Him that you receive His precious Holy Spirit now, and thank Him for it.

> And they were all filled [that is, diffused throughout their being] with the Holy Spirit and began to speak in other tongues (different languages), as the Spirit was giving them the ability to speak out [clearly and appropriately].
>
> **ACTS 2:4 AMP**

Allow me to assist you in speaking what Holy Spirit has revealed, as I speak out loud what he has spoken, and continue to speak to me. He allows these blessings to keep coming about, as the words keep coming out my mouth. You will receive, and continue to receive, all God's blessings that you keep speaking out. Notice, I said that you keep speaking out. You receive what you say, not what someone else say, or pray on you. So stop thinking someone praying against you. I'm giving you a format to follow, of course you can speak what you want, even though I've given you this format. What you speak has already been done by grace through faith. All God's promises are yes and Amen. Remember to say yes, agree knowing it's already done, by grace through faith, as God keeps making a way. Now, receive all these decrees. Don't forget to tell Him thanks!

> For as many as are the promises of God, in Christ they are [all answered] "Yes." So through Him we say our "Amen" to the glory of God.
>
> **2 CORINTHIANS 1:20 AMP**

I'm no longer wanting to receive, I'm receiving now. I'm writing this book to show you how. This was a lesson God had to teach me by way of Holy Spirit. As I write this small book, I pray you receive big blessings. You can be safe, secure, and solid in this large, spacious place He has set you in. Know that with Him you always win.

> When you enter, you will come to people [feeling] safe and secure with a spacious land [widely extended on all sides]; for God has given it into your hands—a place where there is no lack of anything that is on the earth.
>
> **JUDGES 18:10 AMP**

I've seen lack and not enough. I've seen people sick, confused, hurting, resentful, and afraid, to name a few. What about you? I've chosen to speak what God's Word said in this scripture:

> Now to Him who is able to [carry out His purpose and] do superabundantly more than all that we dare ask or think [infinitely beyond our greatest prayers, hopes, or dreams], according to His power that is at work within us,"
>
> **EPHESIANS 3:20 AMP**

What are Decrees?

Speaking what you want and not what you don't want. Commanding God's promises to manifest in your life and not what the enemy speaks to you. Calling God's favor to shine through you.
See below these 5 things about Decrees.

FIVE THINGS ABOUT DECREES

1) We always decree out loud.

2) Decree is about authority.

3) Decrees help establish God's will on the earth through those who decree and declare His Word.

4) When we decree prosperity, we cut in half and slice poverty with a two edge sword.

5) When we decree, we set on fire God's plan to burn on earth, and cause His glory to be manifested.

Learn more about Decrees and what the scripture says about them:

> You will also decide and decree a thing, and it will be established for you; And the light [of God's favor] will shine upon your ways.
>
> **JOB 22:28 AMP**

> Death and life are in the power of the tongue, And those who love it and indulge it will eat its fruit and bear the consequences of their words.
>
> **PROVERBS 18:21 AMP**

Decrees can be spoken out loud, more times, and there's no limit to how many. Whatever the need, you can speak these decrees. Whatever you desire, you must know what's required. Say what God say. Do things His way.

> I know that His commandment is eternal life. So the things I speak, I speak [in accordance with His exact instruction,] just as the Father has told Me.
>
> **JOHN 12:50 AMP**

> The dead do not praise the LORD, Nor do any who go down into silence;
>
> **PSALM 115:17 AMP**

Trust, believe, obey, and do what His Word says, and never go astray; and watch God bring His promises, promotions, provisions, peace, and prosperity to you always. You must have faith to believe what you are speaking according to His Word. Know His Word never returns void.

> So will My word be which goes out of My mouth; It will not return to Me void (useless, without result), Without accomplishing what I desire, And without succeeding in the matter for which I sent it.
>
> **ISAIAH 55:11 AMP**

You must know that the words you speak God hears, and will do what you say.

> Now tell them this: 'As surely as I live, declares the Lord, I will do to you the very things I heard you say.
>
> **Numbers 14:28 NLT**

Let's read and confess these scriptures out loud because God says ask for what we want, which means not in silence. Pay close attention to **1 John 5:14-15 AMP** it uses the word ask three times. When we abide in Him and His Word abide in us, we can ask Him, and whatever His will is; it's done for us. That being said, receive what you've read.

> If you remain in Me and My words remain in you [that is, if we are vitally united and My message lives in your heart], ask whatever you wish and it will be done for you.
>
> **JOHN 15:7 AMP**

> This is the [remarkable degree of] confidence which we [as believers are entitled to] have before Him: that if we ask anything according to His will, [that is, consistent with His plan and purpose] He hears us. And if we know [for a fact, as indeed we do] that He hears and listens to us in whatever we ask, we [also] know [with settled and absolute knowledge] that we have [granted to us] the requests which we have asked from Him.
>
> **1 JOHN 5:14-15 AMP**

We are His body of baptized believers. We are His servants, the chosen, commissioned, and the called out ones, by Him. We must know we are receiving for His purpose.

See below what His purpose is for us:

The Great Commission.

> Now the eleven disciples went to Galilee, to the mountain which Jesus had designated. And when they saw Him, they worshiped Him; but some doubted [that it was really He]. Jesus came up and said to them, "All authority

> (all power of absolute rule) in heaven and on earth has been given to Me. Go therefore and make disciples of all the nations [help the people to learn of Me, believe in Me, and obey My words], baptizing them in the name of the Father and of the Son and of the Holy Spirit, teaching them to observe everything that I have commanded you; and lo, I am with you always [remaining with you perpetually—regardless of circumstance, and on every occasion], even to the end of the age.
>
> **MATTHEW 28:16-20 AMP**

Remember to seek God's Kingdom first, His righteousness, and never worry, because everything you desire has been added unto you.

> But first and most importantly seek (aim at, strive after) His kingdom and His righteousness [His way of doing and being right—the attitude and character of God], and all these things will be given to you also.
>
> **MATTHEW 6:33 AMP**

Know that because of His Kingdom that has come, it's done, and we can live on earth as it is in heaven.

> Your kingdom come, Your will be done On earth as it is in heaven.
>
> **MATTHEW 6:10 AMP**

We must speak what He has said, is saying, and continue to say everyday; and this assures us that all His blessings shall keep coming our way. We must pray, say, stay, and obey what God has spoken in His scriptures.

> If you are willing and obedient, You shall eat the best of the land;
>
> **ISAIAH 1:19 AMP**

LETS START DECREEING AND RECEIVING!

1) Saved/Delivered

- ✝ I decree that because I'm saved and delivered from the enemy, I'm positioned where God wants me to be.
- ✝ I decree my eyes are enlighten, and I see what God wants me to see.
- ✝ I decree that I'm free, and there can never be any chains holding me.
- ✝ I decree that I'm saved, sanctified and filled with His Holy Spirit.
- ✝ I decree that I'm spirit lead and spirit fed.
- ✝ I decree that I have power over the devil.
- ✝ I decree that I've been elevated to new levels.

2) Sanctification/Divine

- ✝ I decree I live in sanctification all the time, as I shine, and walk in His Divine.

✝ I decree that because of my sanctification, I speak to and I pray for the nations.

✝ I decree that because of my sanctification, I'm divinely connected to resurrection power, and I can't be stopped; I keep giving God everything I got.

✝ I decree that I've been set apart, it's because of His love, I will never depart: I know this because He loved me first from the start.

And this, so that I may know Him [experientially, becoming more thoroughly acquainted with Him, understanding the remarkable wonders of His Person more completely] and [in that same way experience] the power of His resurrection [which overflows and is active in believers], and [that I may share] the fellowship of His sufferings, by being continually conformed [inwardly into His likeness even] to His death [dying as He did];

PHILIPPIANS 3:10 AMP

and [as to His divine nature] according to the Spirit of holiness was openly designated to be the Son of God with power [in a triumphant and miraculous way] by His resurrection from the dead: Jesus Christ our Lord.

ROMANS 1:4 AMP

3) Sin/Destroyed

- ✝ I decree I have power over sin, and I can never be destroyed. I now know that sin was a decoy. I live my life full of joy.
- ✝ I decree my life will never be the same, I continue to live in Jesus Name.
- ✝ I decree I fear the Name of the Lord and His Glory at all times; and when the enemy shall come in like a flood, the Spirit of the Lord shall lift up a standard against him.

4) Sickness/Disease

- ✝ I decree I have power over sickness and disease. I'm healed and made whole. I'm healed because God sent His Word and healed. My disease was revealed and now I'm released; no sickness can return to me.
- ✝ I decree I do what it takes in the natural, for my body to remain in its state of health and wholeness statue.
- ✝ I decree that I live long and I live strong. Sickness and disease you don't belong.

5) Satan/Devil

- ✝ I decree I have power over satan and the devil, as I have reached higher levels.

- ✝ I decree I'm restored, rescued, redeemed, resting, ruling, reigning, remaining, and receiving, all my promises that have already been given me, from God by grace through faith.
- ✝ I decree He keeps making away, even when it looks like there is no way. All His blessings are here to stay.
- ✝ I decree I will not go astray, I always follow God's will and His Word every day: as all His blessings keep coming to me day by day.

This part of book deserves more decrees because it speaks from Jesus himself.

6) Savior/Drawing

- ✝ I decree that I keep lifting up Jesus Christ my Savior, on this earth, so that all men are drawn to Him; and I always receive from the Spirit realm.
- ✝ I decree in Christ Jesus I reign, I walk in newness of life, and I'm a living sacrifice.
- ✝ I decree in Christ Jesus I am alive unto God, I continue to bring forth fruit unto Him, that will never depart, and because of this, we all live large.
- ✝ I decree in Christ Jesus I have no condemnation, I have been made free from the law of sin and death, and I keep loving myself.

- ✞ I decree in Christ Jesus nothing can separate me from God's love, this love that has been sent from heaven above.
- ✞ I decree in Christ Jesus I live right, and I always walk in the light.
- ✞ I decree in Christ Jesus my light shines before all mankind, and I receive everything that's mine.
- ✞ I decree that God gets the glory, as the world sees, and receives from my testimony.
- ✞ I decree in Christ Jesus I live, I move, I breathe, and I have my total being.

7) Spirit/Deepest

- ✞ I decree that God has revealed all things to me by His Spirit; and His Spirit has searched out everything and shown me His deepest secrets.
- ✞ I decree I live for Him only, and I have no regrets.
- ✞ I decree that my eyes haven't seen all that God has manifested to me yet, and I'm excited to see what's next.
- ✞ I decree I will never fail any tests.

8) Souls/Driven

- ✞ I decree that souls are driven from the north, south, east, and the west, to become God's very best.

I decree, call, compel, and command, all the lost souls to come, because of Christ Jesus they have won.

I decree that the lost souls won't resist the words spoken by me, they receive their salvation, as I give the invitation.

9) Signs/Display

- ✞ I decree that I'm a sign and a wonder. God has given me everything. God has given me His plans of prosperity.
- ✞ I decree that I have my expected end, I win, and I drive in.
- ✞ The gates are open. God has spoken.
- ✞ I decree that all the enemy's curses are broken.
- ✞ I decree that all my ups always outlast my downs. God is always around. I never have to frown.
- ✞ God has allowed me to smile, even when the road got rough, I'm tough, and I'm built to last.
- ✞ I'm strong in the Lord, and in the power of His might.
- ✞ In Christ Jesus I never loose sight. I love God with all my might.
- ✞ I know that in the times of famine, I'm always satisfied with the fatness, and fruits of the land.
- ✞ I decree that my finances increases everyday.

- ✝ I decree God is allowing this manifestation to keep coming my way. I obey everyday, in every way.
- ✝ I decree that my senses are tuned into His channels.
- ✝ My mind is alert to the things of God. I never fail or fall.
- ✝ I'm on track and making tracks.
- ✝ I decree that people follow me, because I follow Him.
- ✝ I decree that people are saved by the word of God that I speak.
- ✝ I know that God's word is alive and in me.
- ✝ I see and say what He say.
- ✝ My speaking is in line with the light that shines through me, and people see the God in me.
- ✝ I decree that my love for God, causes people to love Him.
- ✝ I decree that wisdom, wealth, and His Word is being heard.
- ✝ I decree that when I speak, wisdom speaks.
- ✝ I decree that my wealth causes people to see and receive His Word, which continues to be heard.
- ✝ Instructions are the key to receive the keys to the Kingdom.

God's Decrees, Spoken By Me, I Receive!

- ✞ I'm no longer looking in from the outside. I live from the inside out.
- ✞ I decree that my inner man continues to stand.
- ✞ I decree there's no struggle, stress, or strain.
- ✞ I know that God has allowed me to gain and remain.
- ✞ I decree that my giving has reached new levels, and I have power over devils.
- ✞ I decree that I rule, rest, reign, and remain, in Jesus name.
- ✞ I never stop, because moving is key.
- ✞ I won't stand still in the storm, because I know where my help comes from.
- ✞ I say action isn't a fraction; and I never have to figure it out.
- ✞ I know that God has already allowed the blessings to come about.
- ✞ I decree that I keep obeying, praying, and staying.
- ✞ I'm in this place of promises, provisions, promotions, and prosperity, that's all for me.
- ✞ I receive it all by grace through faith.
- ✞ I decree that increase keeps coming my way, it's here to stay, and I shall never stray.
- ✞ I decree that Hurricane Harvey has brought my harvest.

- ✝ I know that my seeds don't just meet my needs; they bring increase.
- ✝ I decree that my desires are God's desires for me.
- ✝ I know I'm connected and I will continue to receive the harvest, because of my seeds sown.
- ✝ I have received everything God wants me to own.
- ✝ I decree that I will continue living in this wealthy place that God has me in.
- ✝ I decree there's no place I will fail, the Angels has delivered my mail, there's so much money, that it has tipped over the scale.
- ✝ I decree that the windows of Heaven blessings keeps pouring out, and there's not enough room to receive.
- ✝ I receive all this money that shall continue to come to me.
- ✝ The Kingdom of God is at hand. The Kingdom of God shall continue to stand.
- ✝ I'm open to receive all that God has for me.
- ✝ I receive Now! I thank you God for bringing it all about!
- ✝ I decree that my hands are anointed, and everything I touch increases.
- ✝ I decree that my hands are blessed, and I will never receive mess.

God's Decrees, Spoken By Me, I Receive!

- ✝ I decree my hands are clean, my heart is pure, my service is to God first, and then I can serve man.
- ✝ I receive everything in His plans.
- ✝ I receive and follow instructions that He's given me.
- ✝ I decree that I reach, teach, and preach what Holy Spirit speaks in me, through me, and for me.
- ✝ I decree that I never let go of what I know.
- ✝ God allows me to be a show.
- ✝ I decree that through my wealth, people will see God in my life.
- ✝ I decree that people will pay attention to God's goodness.
- ✝ I decree that they will want to know what to do to receive, all this prosperity He's given me.
- ✝ Thank God, I never gave into what I went through.
- ✝ I had no doubt that He would bring me out.
- ✝ We were rescued! Look at what God can do, and has done.
- ✝ I keep praising! Even right now, I'm shouting as I'm writing!
- ✝ To God be the glory! For all the things He's done!

10) Supernatural/Dominion

- ✝ I keep receiving all that God has already placed in our hands.

- ✞ When the enemy tried to come in like a flood, we continued to stand. I decree I keep moving at God's command.
- ✞ God has truly blessed man and woman!
- ✞ What you saw before, know that God will continue to bless us with even more.
- ✞ God's decrees, there's plenty more in store.
- ✞ Never shut the door that God has opened.
- ✞ Know that in Christ Jesus, and through His Holy Spirit, God has spoken.

Blessed [fortunate, prosperous, and favored by God] is the man who does not walk in the counsel of the wicked [following their advice and example], Nor stand in the path of sinners, Nor sit [down to rest] in the seat of scoffers (ridiculers). But his delight is in the law of the LORD, And on His law [His precepts and teachings] he [habitually] meditates day and night. And he will be like a tree firmly planted [and fed] by streams of water, Which yields its fruit in its season; Its leaf does not wither; And in whatever he does, he prospers [and comes to maturity].

PSALM 1:1-3 AMP

Conclusion

I shall continue to possess what I speak. This little book of decrees will keep bringing big and bountiful blessings to me.

I'm glad you have chosen to speak these decrees with me.

Now, I ask you these questions?

If your answers to all these questions are yes, then you shall continue to be blessed, and receive God's best.

1. Will you receive with me?
2. Will you thank God with me?
3. Will you speak what you want and not what you don't want?
4. Will you speak the blessings and not the curses?
5. Will you speak positive and not negative?
6. Will you say what Jesus says?
7. Will you allow these blessings to keep coming your way everyday?
8. Will you give to help build up God's Kingdom?
9. Will you always obey what God say?
10. Will you hear, listen, and do all that God commanded you?

I trust your answers are all yes.

I decree that you live life full of faith, fruitfulness, flooding in finances, focused, and always having finishing fortitude, allowing Holy Spirit to feed and lead you.

I command the angels to go and bring you everything!

I decree this is the beginning of God's never ending blessings, already done, by grace through faith.

I decree He keeps making a way.

I decree His blessings are here to stay.

I decree you always obey what He continues to say. Blessings Always!

If you enjoyed this book, please check out Lady Mary's other books:

The Secrets Are Out: Nothing Happens Until the Secrets Are Revealed! This powerful and awesome book will allow you to live and love life. Even though you might face troubled situations in life, God has allowed you to know what His Word says about it. You can come through everything that comes against you, when you obey what He says to do. God's secrets revealed are for you to rest, reign, rule, remain, and receive.

Book of Revelations: Divine Disclosures of Best Kept Secrets!: This is another awesome book of revealed secrets from God, which He has blessed me to write, and I know it will bless the body of Christ. Believers must believe these two key truths: 1) God is NOT a man. 2) God DOES NOT lie.

T.S.I.T.S.: Things Seen in the Spirit: God is so awesome! He has allowed me to hear from Him like never before. As I pray daily and communicate with God and begin to listen to Him; He shares secrets with me to be revealed to the world. First God speaks what He wants to happen, how He wants it done and who He wants to do His work.

Confessions Journal: God's Word Spoken in Faith, Believing, that He Will Bring it to Pass According to His Will for Our Lives: Lady Mary Hatter's writing will inspire you, as she shares secrets from God through confessions spoken to her by His Spirit... Confessions from this book will help you to receive everything you want in the Kingdom and everything you want in every area of your life, your family and friend's lives.

Invite Christian Teacher
Lady Mary Hatter
to speak at your church or event

Lady Mary helps people walk in their purpose; which is to build up the Kingdom of God first, and then they can live effective, efficient, and excellent lives, in order to experience all that God has already promised them.

Life Coaching and Author Coaching services are also available.

Follow her on social media:

Facebook: Upe Deisgns Tsits

Twitter: @LadyMaryHatter

Amazon: Click her author page and follow her

To book Lady Mary, please call
281.254.5994

or visit her website and fill out the contact form.

www.MaryHatter.com

www.ingramcontent.com/pod-product-compliance
Lightning Source LLC
Chambersburg PA
CBHW050205130526
44591CB00034B/2157